WIDE AND NARROW

Tom Hughes

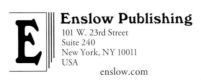

Enslow Publishing
101 W. 23rd Street
Suite 240
New York, NY 10011
USA
enslow.com

Published in 2017 by Enslow Publishing, LLC.
101 W. 23rd Street, Suite 240, New York, NY 10011

Library of Congress Cataloguing-in-Publication Data
Names: Hughes, Tom, 1980- author.
Title: Wide and narrow / Tom Hughes.
Description: New York, NY, USA : Enslow Publishing, LLC, [2017] | Series: All about opposites |
Audience: Ages 5 up. | Audience: Pre-school, excluding K. | Includes bibliographical references and index.
Identifiers: LCCN 2016022980| ISBN 9780766081208 (library bound) | ISBN 9780766081178 (pbk.) |
ISBN 9780766081192 (6-pack)
Subjects: LCSH: Size perception—Juvenile literature. | Size judgment—Juvenile literature.
Classification: LCC BF299.S5 H845 2017 | DDC 153.7/52—dc23
LC record available at https://lccn.loc.gov/2016022980

Printed in China

To Our Readers: We have done our best to make sure all websites in this book were active and appropriate when we went to press. However, the author and the publisher have no control over and assume no liability for the material available on those websites or on any websites they may link to. Any comments or suggestions can be sent by e-mail to cusomterservice@enslow.com

Contents

Words to Know

canoe   elephant   sign

Wide and narrow are opposites.

A highway is wide.

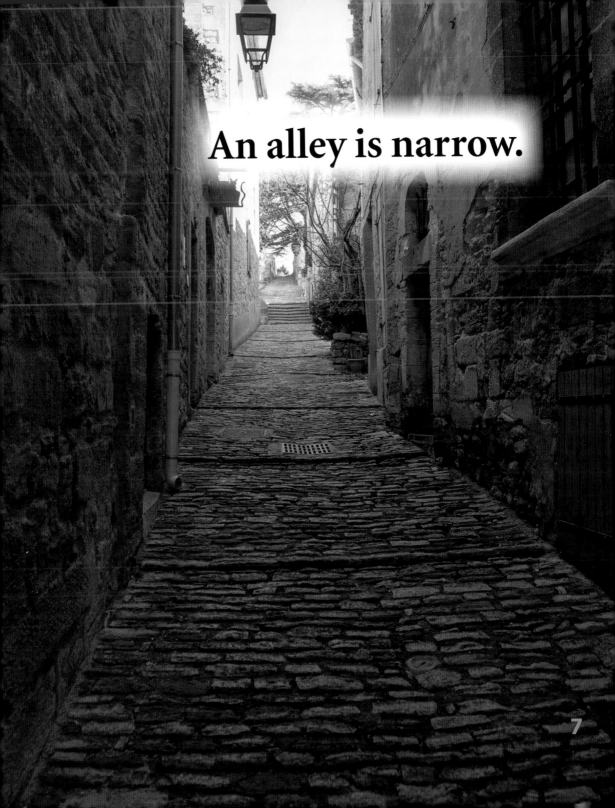

An alley is narrow.

An elephant is wide.

A meerkat is narrow.

Trucks can be wide.

Cars can be narrow.

Some houses are wide.

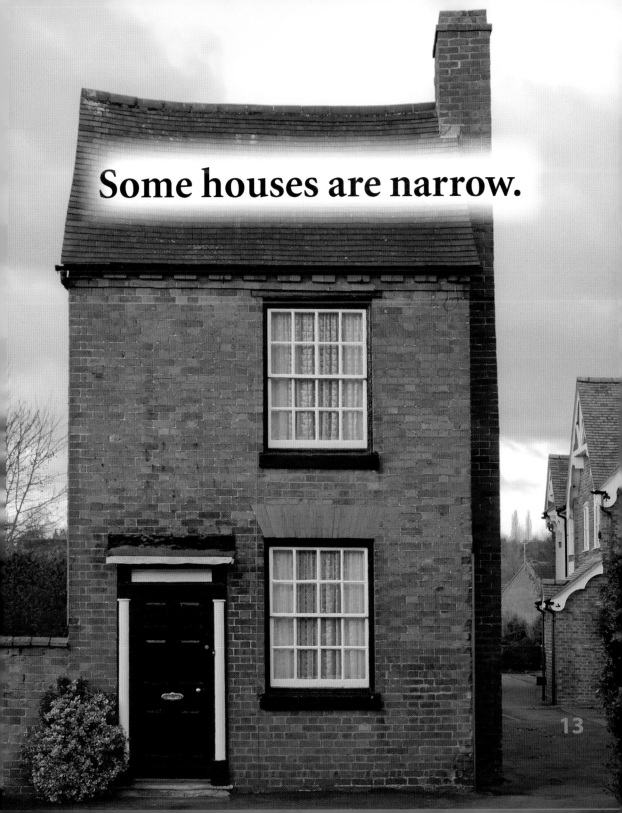

Some houses are narrow.

A wide parking space is easy to get into and leave.

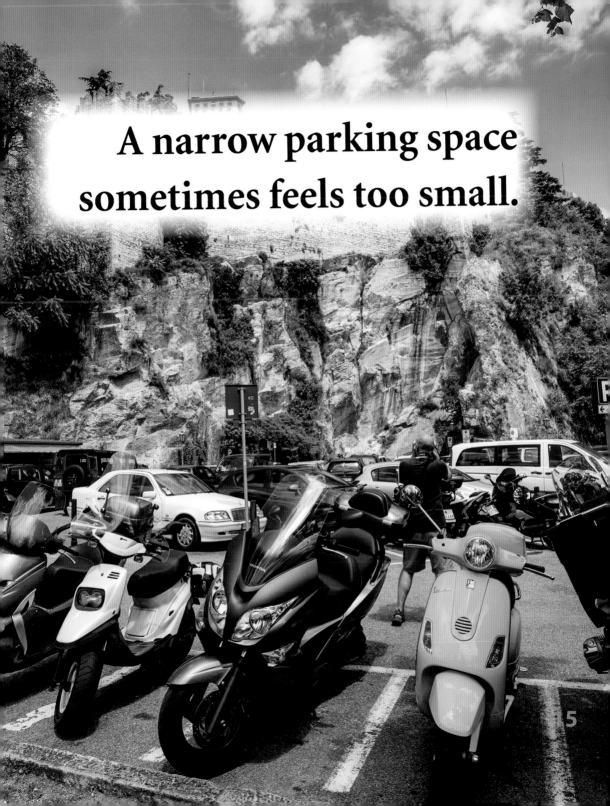

A narrow parking space sometimes feels too small.

5

A river is wide.

A creek is narrow.

A ship is wide.

A canoe is narrow.

Some signs are wide.

Some signs are narrow.

Broadway

DEPT OF TRANSPORTATION

Wide and narrow are important opposites.

Read More

Horacek, Petr. *Animal Opposites*. Somerville, MA: Candlewick Press, 2013.

Katz, David Bar. *Super Heroes Book of Opposites* (DC Super Heroes). New York, NY: Downtown Bookworks, 2013.

Websites

A Game of Opposites
www.meddybemps.com/opposites/Index.html
See if you can match the opposites!

SesameStreet.org
www.sesamestreet.org/videos?video=9fec40f2-156a-11dd-bb51-597ab51d2e81
Learn more about opposites

Index

Guided Reading Level: C
Guided Reading Leveling System is based on the guidelines recommended by Fountas and Pinnell.

Word Count: 86